Spiritual Scientific Healing

Better Health, Greater Wealth, Love and Creative Expression

By:

Jed B. Zimmerman

Mind Matters Inc.

www.mindmattersinc.biz

Published by Mind Matters Inc.

www.mindmattersinc.biz

ISBN 978-0-6151-5552-4

Dedication

This book is dedicated to Dr. P.P. Quimby.

One of the founding fathers of the

New Thought movement.

He lived and practiced Spiritual Scientific Healing.

"Man's happiness is within himself. What we believe, that we create. But this is a truth: A belief may be changed".[1]

http://www.ppquimby.com/index.html

To Dr. Ernest Holmes, founder of the Science of

Mind teaching, for having the Wisdom and the

dedication in sharing with us, Spiritual Truth.
http://www.rsintl.org/

And I would like to acknowledge my friend,

Preston Johnson, who taught me about "The
Mirror".http://www.prestontjohnson.com/

---

[1] The Healing Wisdom of P.P. Quimby, 1982

Table of Contents

Table of Contents

Table of Contents

Spiritual Scientific Healing

is a proven formula for healing that you can use. You **Recognize your Spiritual nature**.

This is your **Higher Power**, where you receive inspiration and guidance.

Through Recognition and the remaining four steps in the formula, direction is given through the **Law of Mind**, the subconscious side of your being, to your thoughts, feelings, emotions and choices, to provide for you, the life you desire.

Webster's dictionary defines healing "as the act or process of curing or restoring to health".

A healing restores wholeness.

Wholeness is a healing in all aspects of one's being.

Better Health, Greater Wealth, Love and Creative Expression can also be yours.

Spiritual Scientific Healing Formula can be found in its entirety on page 98.

Living in the Moment exercise can be found on page 37.

This exercise will help you refocus on being in the present moment. Our issues in life are greatly due to us not Living in the Moment.

We are always fearful of what the future will bring.

This is known as anxiety. We continue to dwell in our past. This prevents us from fully living the present moment. For some, the unchangeable past is a constant torment.

Connecting with your **Higher Power** and being conscious of your breath is the only way that I know of to Live in the Moment.

Journey

We are all on a Journey through this thing called Life. I think of it as the **University of Life**.

How do we pass all the tests and graduate? Well, I don't believe we ever graduate.

As a result of our choices, we just move from one set of circumstances to the next. We evolve!

Why are some people happier than others, wealthier than others, healthier than others and more loving and creative than others?

I believe it is because they have discovered the **Principles of Life** and figured out how to apply them.

These Principles are the **Spiritual Scientific Healing Principles**.

Enjoy the journey!

About the Author

Hello, my name is Jed B. Zimmerman.

I have been a student of Metaphysics since the 60's.

Metaphysics is the study of the Principles that govern our Universe. From my perspective these are **Spiritual Scientific Healing Principles**.

According to Webster's dictionary,

Metaphysics is "the branch of philosophy that deals

with first principles and seeks to explain the nature

of being or reality and of the origin and structure of

the universe".

My first experience with Metaphysics was when my

parents dragged me to hear a mid-week lecture by

Dr. Norman Lunde, a Minister from Religious Science International, also called Science of Mind.

(Not to be confused with Scientology)

As a result of a sports injury, I was on crutches. After attending the lecture I walked out without the use of the crutches.

I have been studying Metaphysics ever since.

There are **no coincidences**.

Everything in your life and mine happens for a reason. I am a graduate student of Religious Science International. This was a four year intensive study program, similar to college. In order to graduate, I had to write a Thesis.

Mine was entitled, "Man's survival in the 90's".

Religious Science taught me Who and What I AM.

I was an active participant in Kundalini Yoga for a number of years.

http://www.kundaliniyoga.com/

I have read and studied Kabbalah.

http://www.kabbalah.com/

It is your Divine Birthright to have a great life.

To enjoy Perfect Health;

To have great abundance and Prosperity;

To have loving relationships in your life,

and to creatively express your highest potential.

It Really Works

In March, 1985, I felt like I was at rock bottom in my life. Emotionally, I was a basket case. I felt like my life had fallen apart.

I used the **Spiritual Scientific Healing Formula**, and **declared** that the right and perfect woman show up in my life. The next week, I met my wife, AnnMarie, and moved in with her two weeks later. Twenty two years have

passed and we are still together. The icing on the cake is that we met on the Anniversary of her Mother's passing.

I give thanks to my wife, AnnMarie for her loving support, and for giving me the time and space to discover myself. AnnMarie has helped with the editing of this book, as well as discussing and giving me her perspective.

Spirit - Soul - Body

As human beings, we are comprised of three distinct parts; **Spirit, Soul** and **Body.**

"Man is a threefold principle of life and action; he is Spirit, Soul and Body. From the Spirit he receives inspiration and guidance; in the Soul he finds a perfect Law of life; and through the body he proves that he is a real individualization of the Invisible Principle".[2]

Spirit - God, Conscious Mind, Absolute. We get inspiration, guidance and intuition.

Soul – Subconscious, Subjective, Law of Mind, Karma, Race Conscious thinking.

Body – Physical body, ego, effects, material world, form, conditions, The Mirror, time, space.

A harmonious synthesis of these three parts is what is needed to live a full and balanced life.

---

[2] Dr. Ernest Holmes, Religious Science, The Science of Mind textbook 1938

Spiritual Scientific Healing Principles

Remember the boomerang?

"The most recognizable type is the returning boomerang, a kind of Throwing Stick that, when thrown correctly, travels in a curved path and returns to its point of origin".[3]

What did the Boomerang do when we through it out?

It came back. This is a **Principle of life**.

Whatever you put out into the Universe, it will come back to you. This Principle may be more familiar to you as, **"whatever goes around, comes around"**.

Principles are absolute- they always work.

If you put out anger, hate, distrust….. This is what will come back. The same is true for Love, kindness and compassion.

---

[3] http://en.wikipedia.org/wiki/Boomerang

Cause and Effect

Everything that you do is based on your **choices**.

What you do or say to others you do to yourself.

Everything that is going on in your life is a result of

choices that you have made.

Choice starts the wheels of **Cause and Effect**.

Webster's Dictionary definition-

Cause-"something that brings about a result.

A person or a thing that is the agent of bringing something

about".

Effect- "result, consequence, outcome.

Everything which we see, touch, taste, feel, hear or

sense with the physical senses is an effect".

Our entire material world is an effect.

"Cause and Effect are really one, and if we have a given cause set in motion, the effect will have to equal the cause. One is the inside and the other, the outside of the same thing".

"A certain, specific, intelligent idea in Mind, will produce a certain, specific, concrete manifestation equal to itself". "If man takes his images of thought only from his previous experiences, then he continues in the bondage which those previous experiences create." [4]

---

[4] Dr. Ernest Holmes, Religious Science, The Science of Mind textbook 1938

Judgment

When you judge, you become the judged. The
Master teacher said it this way,

**"Judge not that ye be not judged, for with what
judgment ye judge, ye shall be judged, and with
what measure ye mete, it shall be measured to you
again"**.[5]

We are here to love ourselves and everyone else who
comes into our life, unconditionally, without
Judgment, without Judgment. I can't say this
enough. You must love yourself unconditionally.
You cannot give love to anyone else if you don't love
yourself first.

This Spiritual Scientific Healing Principle is really
the same as Cause and Effect. If you put judgment out,
judgment comes back.

---

[5] King James Bible, (Matt. 7:1,2)

Law of Attraction

Have you heard about the movie called The Secret?

It is based on the **Spiritual Scientific Healing Principle, the Law of Attraction.**

Whatever you believe, whatever you dwell on with your thoughts, feelings and emotions will be attracted into your life.

"Every person is surrounded by a thought atmosphere. This mental atmosphere is the direct result of his conscious and unconscious thought, which, in its turn, becomes the direct reason for, and the cause of, that which comes into his life.

Through this power we are either attracting or repelling. Like attracts like and it is also true that we may become attracted to something which is greater than our previous experience, by first embodying the atmosphere of our desire". [6]

---

[6] . Ernest Holmes, Religious Science, The Science of Mind textbook 1938

Law of Circulation

This is the Law of **giving and receiving**.

You must give, in order to receive.

Giving comes in many different forms: money, time,

energy, love, food, barter. The forms are only limited

by the imagination.

Learn how to give graciously without expecting

anything in return.

The Universe will not let you down.

The tighter you hold onto something, the more likely

you are to lose it. Relax, and share your good.

It will be returned and multiplied.

Law of Correspondence

You must provide a **mental equivalent** of your

desires for them to manifest in your life.

This is sometime referred to as providing a

"**spiritual prototype**". You must know what you

want before it will manifest. You must think about it,

feel what you want with strong emotion.

See it in your mind's eye as already being done.

Use your powers of creative visualization and imagery.

Create a **Treasure Map** of what you want

your life to look like. Use a poster board and cut

things out from magazines or use visuals of whatever

resembles what you want. Paste these onto your poster board.

This will give you something to look at that will help

you visualize the desired result.

Law of Averages

You don't hear too many people talking about this one. It is important. I am not even sure this is a Law, but I know it to be a **Truth**.

It states that you can rise above the crowd. That you don't have to follow the masses. You don't have to buy into the opinions of the world. Because that is just what they are, opinions. When you rise above the crowd, you walk your own path and discover **Who** you are.

When you do this, and align yourself with the **Spiritual Scientific Healing Principles**, you will have less melodrama in your life.

Now, please be clear. I am not saying you will no longer be affected by life's issues. What I am saying is that you will be in charge of your life. You will be consciously giving your life direction, by your thoughts, feelings, emotions and then by the choices you make.

As a result of being conscious, you will recognize what your **beliefs** are. You will start to examine them. Those that no longer suit you will be replaced by **beliefs** that are in accord with what you **Do** want, not what you Do Not want.

Our senses are bombarded with opinions and untruths. How do we know what **Truth** is and what is opinion? I get the comment all the time, that what my truth is might not be anyone else's truth.

Hogwash!

The **Spiritual Scientific Healing Principles**

that you are reading about in this book are **Not** mine.

Whose are they? Well, I would say they are built into the Universe by **God.**

The bottom line is when you hear a **Truth**, you **Know** it. It **resonates** with you. You will hear the same thing over and over again from anyone on the **Spiritual** path. All the rest are opinions.

And opinions are subject to change.

Principle of Forgiveness

This is so important! We all have so many hurts that
we have picked up along the way of living. The act of
Forgiving is a necessity to moving forward.

We can't move forward in **Love** if we are holding on
to thoughts, feelings and emotions of anger or hate
or jealousy or revenge or…etc.

Please forgive yourself first, without judging yourself.
There is no need to add blame.
And then please forgive those that have hurt you. If
they are alive and you are able to talk with them,
ask them to forgive you. If this is too painful, write
them a note and either mail it to them or rip it up.

Principle of Surrender or Release

When you have completed forgiveness, then
it is time to move forward.

The way to get closure is to **Surrender** or **Release**
into **Law** or Universal Mind, to **God**.
It is an action, a movement of thought, feeling
and emotion that now is complete.
I have seen people release balloons in the air to
symbolize Release.

Get a bottle that will float and write out a
Spiritual Scientific Healing. Put your message in
the bottle and release it into the ocean.

Be creative; it can be symbolic.

Principle of Gratitude or Thanksgiving

If you want more blessings in your life, then give

thanks for what you already have.

If you can't think of anything to be thankful or

grateful for, then give thanks for your **breath of**

life. For without this, you would not be here reading these

words.

Develop the **consciousness of gratefulness,**

the **attitude of gratitude**.

When you do this, the Universe will lavish you with all you

desire. We truly have much to be thankful for.

I am reminded of this, each time I talk with someone

about their life.

Who are You?

We are all **Spiritual Beings**! We are the **Beloved**!
We are **created in the image and the likeness of
God.** And so are **you**. We have been given the
greatest gift of all, the **Power of Choice**, the Power
to choose what we wish to experience.

"Many Meanings for Divine Guidance can come from
many sources. Yet by opening to guidance from the
divine, we open to the support of powerful forces
greater than ourselves". "The divine has different meanings for
different people, whether it be God, Creator, Jehovah, Allah,
or Great Spirit". "Yet even if you don't believe in any of these,
consider the possibility that there is a very wise part of
yourself—a higher self or a deeper self—which can provide
you with guidance. What is important is that we open to this
presence, however we choose to define the divine, and that we
consciously invite this powerful guidance into our daily
lives".[7]

---

[7] Fred Burks- http://www.myspace.com/fredburks

We are all Connected

We are all in the same boat of life, experiencing our humanity through our unique expression.

"There is one mind common to all individual men".[8]

There is a **Power for Good in the Universe**. I call it **God**. The Universe is the physical manifestation of this Creator. Every human being has access to a **Power greater than himself**. This Power is your life now. When you recognize this as being so, you will be on your way to transforming your life.

It is our **Divine Birthright** to have **Good Health, Abundant Wealth, Creative Self Expression** that is satisfying to us, and **Loving Relationships** in our life.

---

[8] Ralph Waldo Emerson

The Miracle of Life

The sun rise and sun set, the ebb and flow of the
oceans. Just think of the healing power within your
body, when you get a cut on your finger.
Think about conception and the birth of babies.

The **Miracle of Life** is all around us.
We take everything for granted! So we need to be
awake, aware and conscious of life and of ourselves.

"Just contemplate the awesome design and balance
within any one family of the animal, vegetable, or
mineral kingdom, to say nothing of the beauty of the
human body or the elegance of the solar system. The
miracle of nature is not to be found in its once-in-a-
lifetime events, but in its relentless regularity".[9]

---

[9] website http://www.meaningfullife.com/

"Whereas every creation of man is ephemeral, every

part of nature is boundless, permanent, and

inexplicable -- in a word, miraculous.

Yes, we can explain away many events, even

"miraculous" ones. But then again, a good mind can

explain away anything. Just as you have a choice in

everything you do, you can use your mind to either seek out

the miracles in life or deny them. Only you

will know the degree of sincerity with which you are

trying to understand your life and instill it with meaning". [10]

---

[10] website http://www.meaningfullife.com/

Separation from our Source

When we are afraid, it is because we feel like we

have **lost our connection** or **feel separated** from our

Source.

As a result, we feel like we have lost control and

start to look **outside** of ourselves for our answers.

When we get that empty feeling, the feeling of

despair, that is an indicator that we feel separated

from our **Source**.

We go to great lengths to reconnect. For the

most part, we are looking in the wrong place.

This is the time to get quiet and get back in touch

with your **Source** of well being. It is **within you**. We

are still in the awakening state of remembering

Who we are. We are the **Beloved**.

We are all **connected**. Know this and Feel it.

We were and are never separated, but we think and feel like we are.

This idea of separation must be changed for you to experience the kind of life that you truly desire. I am not saying to deny what you feel.

It is very important to honor your **feelings**. Just don't stay there. Move through it and see what is there for you to learn about yourself.

We are **Spiritual Beings** having a human experience through our unique expressions.

The greatest gift that we have been given is the **Power of Choice**. The freedom to choose what our life will be like.

The Creative Process

Your **Mind** is the creative power in your life.
Through your thoughts and beliefs about yourself,
you create your world. Your life is the demonstration
of your beliefs about yourself.

What you think about and believe in with strong
emotion, you become!

Not fleeting thoughts, but what you dwell upon with
feeling and conviction, becomes your reality.

Our being **connected**, includes all human beings, and
all living creatures. That is why whatever you say or
do to others comes back to you.

The Mirror

Life is a mirror, reflecting out and back to you what is going on with **you** and no one else. Let all your judgment fall away. This includes first and foremost your judgment of yourself.

What you see in **your** universe is **your** mirror, reflecting back to you, how **you** think and feel about **yourself.**

Live your life Judgment free and give everyone else who comes into your space, **Unconditional Love.** Respect everyone's right to live their life as they see fit **without judgment** from you. What you put out comes back. If you condemn others, you are really condemning yourself.

"What goes around comes around".

We are also the Mirror for other people to get in touch with their **Soul Memory**. This is when we push buttons in others. When others react to your comments and **project onto you their Words** as a judgment, **this judgment is their Mirror**, not yours.

That is why you don't judge others. If you judge them, you become the judged.

"I AM aware that the expression of my life is a perfect mirror of that which I believe. I take the time to assess my priorities and to re-evaluate the world in which I live, for it is a reflection of my innermost thoughts and beliefs." (author unknown)

Do you sabotage yourself with doubts, fears, worry or anxiety? Do you enjoy the moment?

Doubt, Fear, Worry and Anxiety

These four words are killers to your State of
Mind for living in **Peace**, **Love** and **Joy**. When you
are doubting yourself, or worrying about something
in your life, or being afraid, or feeling anxious, then
you are not **Living in the Moment**.

When you are in any of these four states of mind,
you will not have the creativity needed to move forward.

On the next page is the Living in the Moment Exercise, that
will get you back to **Conscious Awareness**, and if you let it, it
will bring back your state of **Peace**, **Love** and **Joy**.

Living in the Moment Exercise

Stay in the Moment, Be here Now!

Remember **Who** you are: You are a **Spiritual**

Being having a human experience. You are the

Beloved, Created in the Image and Likeness of

God. If you embrace nothing else, this idea will transform you.

STOP here, close your eyes; be conscious of your

breath. Breathe deeply and slowly, inhale deeply,

exhale deeply and slowly.

Continue to breathe like this until you feel a quiet

peace come over you. Do Not go further until you

have quieted your breath. You are **God's breath** of

Life, so breathe deeply.

Do this as long as it takes to accomplish an awareness of **Peace** and **Love** within your being.

This is your **Meditative** state that you ALWAYS NEED TO COME BACK TO, to get yourself centered. If you do nothing else, do this exercise.

IT WILL GET YOU THROUGH THE MOMENT. When you are centered and quiet, breathe deeply again, and as you do so, say to yourself, **I AM** the healing energy of **God**. And as you exhale, say to yourself, I let go of all Dis-ease from my Mind, Body, Spirit and Soul.

I let go of all Doubt. I let go of all Fear. I let go of all Worry. I let go of all Anxiety.
I replace these States of Mind with thoughts of **Peace**, **Love**, **Joy** and **Happiness**.

Divine Right Action is now taking over. **I AM Worthy**

and **Deserving** of the very Best of everything that Life has to

offer. I claim my Divine Inheritance, Right Now. With great

Thanksgiving, I release this **Spiritual Scientific**

Healing into Law and say, And so it is.

Doubt, Fear, Worry and Anxiety,

become issues for us when we are not

Living in the Moment.

If you were not able to get your self centered with

your breathing, to do the **Spiritual Scientific Healing**, then

do not lose hope.

The exercise on the next page will also work to get you back to

Living in the Moment.

Be aware of your breathing.

Call attention to it.

I am breathing.

I feel my lungs and my stomach move as I inhale.

Do the same for the exhale.

Then wherever it is that you are, start looking around your physical space, your surroundings, and say out loud what you see. Start with yourself. I am wearing a purple, tank top tee shirt. I have a blue bathing suit on.

Be very specific.

I see my desk. It has two sections. One section is a right angle. This section is where my computer sits. Be very specific. I see my computer. The color of my computer is grey. I have my two wonderful dogs with me………. (Do you get the idea?)

Allow your **Mind** to be **Conscious**, aware

of your surroundings. Say everything that you see

around you and this will bring you back to the

moment.

The **Mind** can only think one thought at a time. Stay in the

moment, be **conscious** of **Who** you are.

 You are the **Beloved**. Be **Grateful** for all your Blessings and

give **Thanks** for them.

 There is a Power for Good in the Universe, this

Power is **God**, and this Power is **Your** life now!

Consciousness

According to Webster's dictionary,

Consciousness is "the state of being conscious; awareness of one's own feelings, what is happening around one, etc. The totality of one's thoughts, feelings, and impressions; conscious mind".

It is through **Conscious Awareness** that we begin to make changes. Be mindful or aware of your thoughts. If you train yourself to listen, you will hear your chatter. My chatter is from my Ego. It is not **Life-Affirming**. This is how I know it is from my Ego.

Webster's dictionary defines Ego as,

"that part of the psyche which experiences the external world, or reality, through the senses, organizes the thought processes rationally, and governs action".

When you hear these thoughts, you can bring yourself back to center and focus on **Life-Affirming** ideas, or **spiritual** ideas.

Conscious and Subconscious

Human beings have **One Mind** with two aspects.

Webster's dictionary definitions state the following.

"**Conscious** is (objective)-aware, known or felt by one's inner self".

"**Subconscious** (subjective)-existing in the Mind and affecting thought and behavior without entering conscious awareness. Mental activities below the threshold of consciousness".

Our thinking, when combined with strong feelings, turn into beliefs, which are automatically filling our subconscious. What we have been programmed with as a child, lies dormant in our subconscious, waiting to be recalled.

"The subjective state of a man's thought decides what is going to happen to him in his objective experience. The subjective state of his thought is the sum total of his thinking and knowing. It is the medium between the Limitless and the conditioned. Whatever is involved in it, will evolve".

"Therefore, when there is no longer anything in our mentality which denies our word, a demonstration will be made; nothing can stop it, for the Law is Absolute".[11]

You determine what's in your subconscious by observing the beliefs that have demonstrated in your life. Everything that is going on in your life is a reflection or confirmation of what you believe about yourself. You can either be consciously aware of it or not.

---

[11] Dr. Ernest Holmes, Religious Science, The Science of Mind textbook 1938

In order for you to have what you truly desire and deserve, the subconscious has to be re-programmed.

Your subconscious does not know anything about the future, it only knows this moment. What does this mean? It means if you want to be a millionaire, then think and act and feel and imagine that you are already are. Think as a millionaire thinks. Believe as a millionaire would believe.

The subconscious must buy into a new reality for you. Action is required to move you forward in fulfilling your desires. When the Universe presents ideas, evaluate and take action.

Where do our Beliefs come from?

SELF-IMAGE

SELF-WORTH

SELF-ESTEEM

Self-image is our over-all perception of how we think and feel about ourselves.

Self-worth is the measure or the criterion we use to determine how much more of life we feel worthy of accepting. This is based on our **consciousness**.

Self–esteem measures our level of confidence.

"Your personal power is measured by how much you believe in yourself. Your faith in yourself establishes your level of consciousness and builds your self-esteem and self-worth."[12]

All three of these are interwoven so well that they all flow together as one.

---

[12] Darel Rutherford, So Why Aren't You Rich? 1998

Who do our Beliefs come from?

As a result of the **Miracle of Life**, we are born.

We hear our parents or siblings or relatives talking

and doing things, and we take into our **consciousness** the

emotional meaning of what we hear and see. I am not

necessarily talking about the everyday, mundane things of life,

but that is included as well.

I am talking about the emotional meaning of their

existence. Are my parents loving to each other? Do

they enjoy their existence? Or are they mean,

hateful people who don't like themselves or anyone else?

Do they show their Love to me? Do they think I am

beautiful and worthy of my existence? Or do they

feel so poorly about themselves that it is tough for

them to provide me with positive loving expression.

Our personality and belief system are formed at a very early age. When we go to school, we pick up all the **race-conscious** beliefs that other people have. This is not about skin color or ethnicity. This is about the subjective or subconscious thoughts of the race.

We get this from our parent's beliefs as well. This is where all the prejudices, hate and ideas of separation come from… that our country is better than theirs, that our religion is better than theirs, etc. This is the basis for all of our Wars.

The **race-conscious** thoughts become part of our belief system, and separates us from our Good. Race conscious thought goes by many names. Race-Mind, Race-Thought, Race-Suggestion.

"This is nothing more than human beliefs operating through the mentality of the individual. The tendency to reproduce what the race has thought and experienced. This race-suggestion is a prolific source of disease. These accumulated subjective tendencies of the human race are operative through any person who is receptive to them". [13]

The only way that I am aware of, for dealing with race-conscious thought is to be aware, conscious of **Who** you are. **You are the Beloved.** You are created in the image and likeness of **God.** This means you are **God's** expression of **Truth, Love, Peace, Harmony, Health, Abundance**, and all the other **Life-Affirming** qualities you can think of. You have been given the power of choice and the power of thought. Think about, feel and believe what will bring joy into your life.

---

[13] Dr. Ernest Holmes, Religious Science, The Science of Mind textbook 1938

False Beliefs

As children, we have been taught false beliefs.

WHY have we been taught false beliefs???

There are numerous answers, some innocent, some

not! Let's start with the innocent. We learn the

false beliefs from our parents because they did not

know any better. This is what they were taught, so it

became their belief system as then ours.

Whether your parents are still alive or not,

don't blame them or judge them or yourself.

Love them and yourself unconditionally.

As you started to grow up and move out into the

world, you absorbed the **race-conscious** thought

from your peers, teachers, priests, rabbis, the

government, etc. The list goes on. Well guess what…

this is how false beliefs get passed down.

Other innocent false Beliefs

Examine the myths, superstitions and old wife's tales that you were raised with.

"If you go out in the rain, you will catch a cold".

"If you touch a frog you will get warts".

"Don't let your cats go around your newborns; they will take their breath away".

"Don't open the umbrella in the house it brings bad luck".

(LUCK=**Logical Use of Conscious Knowledge**)

"Breaking a mirror brings seven years of bad luck".

There are literally hundreds, maybe thousands, of old wife tales. You will be surprised to hear the ones you have grown up with that are not true.

The not so innocent false Beliefs

Power, Greed, how do we keep them down on the farm?
Don't teach them the truth. Keep them in ignorance.

Before I continue with this line of thought, please

remember that we are dealing with a **Power** within

all of us. A Power that can be used for **Peace**, **Love**

and **Joy**. Or a Power that can be used for everything else. We

are dealing with **Principles** and **Laws** that are **immutable**.

Look at the Principle of electricity. We can use electricity for

cooking and heating our home or we can use it to kill

someone.

When we become consciously aware, that "**what**

we put out comes back" to us, then we can make

a choice, to use electricity in a productive way or in a

destructive way.

Let's get back to the not so innocent false beliefs.

We are talking about Power and Greed and a host of

other thoughts that will never, never, bring **Peace** and **Joy**.
We were not taught the truth, about how life is meant to be
lived. As a result, we live under false beliefs.

Why? Because there are people in our Universe, that

don't love themselves. If you don't love yourself, then you
can't give love to anyone else. Where does this come from?
Most likely it is from not feeling good about ourselves.

When we don't have a positive self-image, we start

to feel separate or separated from our Source.
With nothing to ground us, this leads us on a path of
chaos and destruction.

Just as we are given the power of choice in how we

use the principle of electricity, we can choose to

either put out **Love** or put out hate. We have the freedom to
make choices, that always, always, have results.

When we feel separate from our good, or what I choose to call

God, we may be outwardly

successful, but inwardly empty and unfilled. This

disparity changes our motivations for living our life.

The result is that our lives are not based on **Love** or

Joy or living in **Peace**. So we think and act and

conduct ourselves in an opposite manner. Hate,

violence, war, murder, rape… the negative patterns

are endless. Your focus becomes controlling others.

You lie to them, you teach them false beliefs

instead of Universal Truths. You cheat them, you

kill them, and you take advantage of them every

chance you get. You've heard the expression it's a

dog eat dog world and F__k them before they F__k you.

You teach them ignorance! Now were these all conscious

thoughts and acts that have been done since the beginning of

time to take our power away? I believe they were.

They were deliberate.

False Beliefs that do the most damage

We are all sinners!

The real reason we were taught that we are sinners,

is to make us believe that our **Power** lies outside of

ourselves and we that we need someone's approval,

other than ourselves for our salvation, our own

happiness. This is a victim consciousness that we

have accepted throughout the ages.

We are now as a collective consciousness, (group

consciousness), awakening to the fact, that we are

Spiritual Beings.

You can learn more about the victim Consciousness

on page 66.

Sin

The word Sin in the original Aramaic translation of the Bible, is an archery term, meaning to miss the mark. It is basically about **cause and effect**. If you put something out, like an arrow or a comment and it misses the mark or does not accomplish what you wanted it to, make a change in direction and try again. Don't judge yourself for missing the mark.

Just remember it is all about choices.

Make another choice and try again.

God Punishes us for our behavior

I don't believe there is an anthropomorphic (characteristics attributable to a human form) person somewhere in the sky called **God**. I don't believe there is a **God** that sits in judgment on us and doles out punishment or reward based on our behavior.

We do all this to ourselves.

We can change this if we choose to.

"So long as man abides in the conviction that God causes him to suffer, he closes his mind against the inflow of God's gifts of health, peace, and harmony". [14]

---

[14] Metaphysical Bible Dictionary, 1931

Our Power lies outside of us

This false belief is similar to sinners. This belief keeps us as victims. It tells us that we need someone's approval for living our lives.

The only person you need approval from is yourself.

Remember, the **Power resides within** all of us. We align with this Power. When we learn how to use the **Spiritual Scientific Healing Principles**, we can use this **Power for Good** in our life.

It, is based on knowing **Who** we are, aligning with this truth and then giving direction to our Mind, through our thinking, feeling and emotion.

Duality- Heaven and Hell, Good and Evil

If we are not good on Earth, when we die we go to a

place called Hell. Heaven and Hell is the same thing. They are

both states of mind. If you believe your life is Hell, it is. If you

believe your life is Heaven, then it is.

The Master teacher said it this way,

"As thou hast believed so it be done unto thee".[15]

We have come to recognize this as,

"It is done unto you as you believe".

It is what you choose to make it. The belief in Heaven and

Hell is the same Principle as the belief in Good and Evil.

(EVIL spelled backwards is LIVE)

"A belief in duality is a belief in separation from

our Source. We are all Connected Spiritual Beings.

The whole confusion of the world arises from fundamental

errors of thought. Chief among these errors-and the father to a

greater part of the others- IS A BELIEF IN DUALITY. The

belief in duality supposes that evil is equal to good".[16]

---

[15] King James Bible (Matt: 8: 13)

[16] Dr. Ernest Holmes, Religious Science, The Science of Mind textbook 1938

We now live in a Global Village. Because of the Internet, and other popular communications media, we are even more connected than ever before.

Whatever we do, even the smallest gesture that you

put out, will touch others in some way.

Why not try a new approach to live and put out Love, instead of hate and distrust.

False beliefs are based on Fear.

When we continue to live with our **False beliefs**, we

become unempowered. We are not living an

authentic life. We need to be true to our self.

"To thine own self be true, and it must follow, as

the night the day, thou canst not then be false to any man".
William Shakespeare

We need to Suffer to grow

I don't believe this. If you do, then guess what
happens? **"It is done unto you as you believe"**.

So the Universe finds a way to bring the suffering
to you. You will have plenty of opportunities to deal
with life's issues. These issues will give you the
freedom of choice to experience pleasure or pain
and suffering.

Suffering or anything associated with
it, can have a devastating effect on your being,
particularly your body. I am not talking about
grieving for someone. People need to grieve and
have closure for dealing with personal tragedies.
But suffering will be a choice that **You** make.

It is noble to be Poor

I know there is a **Power for good, God,** in my life.
I believe it is my **Divine birthright** to have it all. I
claim the very best of everything.

If **I AM** to believe that **I AM the Beloved** and **I AM**
created in the **image** and **likeness** of **God,** then
why would I believe that it is noble to be poor?

The **Consciousness** of **Prosperity,** of **Abundance**
in all areas of life, is what I believe to be noble.

Empowerment

"To learn how to think is to learn how to live".[17]

Empowerment is taking charge of your life, of your Destiny, through the power of your thinking, feeling, faith and actions. It is realizing **Who** and **What** you are. It is your **consciousness**.

Empowerment is an inside job.
You don't get it from anyone else.
People can inspire you, but no one can make you feel empowered. Don't give your power away; you have a choice. Your true power lies within you. Don't let anyone tell you anything different. Anyone teaching you Truth about Empowerment, won't want to control your power, your money or your possessions.

---

[17] Dr. Ernest Holmes, Religious Science, The Science of Mind textbook 1938

"Imagine for a moment a world where all people truly did their best to love and empower each other. Imagine if a significant number of the people on this planet truly did their best to live by these simple keys. You can choose to become one of those people right now. You can choose to make your life and our world a better place. It is fully possible. There are people of all races, religions, and beliefs around the globe already committed to living by these or similar ideals. Let us then choose with an open mind and heart to add to their numbers. Let us choose every day of our lives to do what's best for all, to open to divine guidance, to accept and understand, and to love and empower ourselves and all around us to be the best that we can be."[18]

---

[18] Fred Burks- http://www.myspace.com/fredburks

How to take Charge of your life

We are **Spiritual Beings** having a human experience. What we think about we become! This is the University of LIFE!

There is a **POWER FOR GOOD** in this Universe, and we can use it to change our lives.

This power lays dormant waiting for your recognition to give it expression, through your thoughts, words and deeds. Through our free will we can reprogram our Mind.

Victim or Creator

When you become Empowered and take
responsibility for your life, your personal creation,
then you no longer will have the **victim consciousness**. You
know, the one - my husband did this to me. My boss did this
to me. My teacher made me feel this way. This is
all about choice. Your creation is based on your
choices- consciously and mostly unconsciously.

"Like it or not, you are given many opportunities in
life to choose to be a victim or to be a creator.
When you choose to be a victim, the world is a cold
and harsh place. "They" did things to you which
caused all of your pain and suffering. "They" are wrong and
bad, and life is rotten as long as "they" are around".
"The essence is that "they" are to blame for all your
problems, because "they" are ruining your life and world. And
the truth is, your life is likely to stay that way as long as you see

"them" as having control and yourself as the powerless victim".

"Victims relish in anger, resentment, revenge, and all sorts of emotions and behaviors that cause others to feel like victims, too. Creators consciously choose love, inspiration, empowerment, and other emotions and behaviors which inspire not only themselves, but all around them to continually create the lives and world they want to live in".

"Yet whether they know it or not, both victim and creator always have choice in each moment to determine the direction of their lives through what they choose to do with what they are given".[19]

19 http://www.weboflove.org/qualityoflife

You Create Your Reality

If you want to become empowered to change your life, your reality, you must first accept responsibility for creating it. Please don't over analyze this.
It is just something we need to embrace first, so we can make changes.

We use such a small portion of our **Mind,** there is much we cannot perceive and do not understand. For the most part we have created our life unconsciously. We were not aware that the choices that we made, turn into conditions, that show up in our lives.

We need to accept responsibility for our creation, without guilt or judgment or blame. We become empowered to change our reality based on new choices we make.

So a new set of **Causes** and **Effects** go into motion by You,

thinking and feeling about what you Do want in your life.

Paint a picture in your Mind's eye of what you want.

Really image it and feel it.

Be what you want and the Universe will bring it your way.

When you have a thought or image contrary to

what you want, negate it. Say this is no longer

the truth about me and bless it and let it go.

Karma – Free Will - Reincarnation

I believe in **Karma**. (the totality of a person's actions in any one of the successive states of that person's existence, thought of as determining the fate of the next stage - Webster's dictionary).

Free Will, (the freedom of the Will to choose a course of action without external coercion but in accordance with the ideals or moral outlook of the individual- Webster's dictionary) I believe that the only time we have **Free Will**, is for the choices that we make in the moment. This of course sets into motion new **Causes** that lead to new **Effects** or conditions.

I believe in **Reincarnation**. (the doctrine that the soul reappears after death in another and different bodily form.-Webster's dictionary)I don't believe that my current incarnation is my first one. And it probably won't be my last. We are all immortal beings, our soul is immortal.

Life Areas

There are four principle **Life Areas** important to everyone. They are **Health, Wealth, Love** and **Creative Expression.**

Whatever is going on for you in any of these areas is a direct manifestation of what you believe about yourself. The **Spiritual Scientific Healing Principles** work the same for all the **Life Areas.**

Let's pick one **Life Area** for us to examine what our beliefs are. Now keep in mind - that life mirrors back to us what we are, based on what we believe about ourselves. But again, most of this comes from our subconscious belief system. It is not until we become aware and accept responsibility for everything in our lives that we become empowered to make changes.

Are you enjoying good health? We deserve to be healthy, to feel good so that we may enjoy our lives.

You might say, I did not choose to be sick or to

have dis-ease in my body. But I believe somewhere in your incarnation path, that you did choose, although maybe not consciously.

I ask you to accept what is in your life this very

moment. It does not matter how it got there, but

just accept your part in the creation process.

What about all the children who are born sick or disabled? I say to you love them **Unconditionally, without judgment**.

There is much we do not know and understand.

When we talk about **Spirit**, there are times that

our words cannot convey the **Truth** or meaning for

our circumstances or experiences.

This is where your **Faith** comes in.

"Faith is the substance of things hoped for, the evidence of things not seen".[20]

The opposite of Faith is fear. (**false evidence appearing real**).

We must have Faith that there is a **Power for Good** for all mankind. There are no accidents, no coincidences. We are all here in the right time and the right place, doing and being. **Love** yourselves and everyone else unconditionally and without judgment. If you are not healthy, not feeling good, figure out a way to find out what you believe about yourself. If you are judgmental, if you have a negative outlook on life and you speak your word with negativity, hostility and venom- then this is a good place to start. You need to be loving, kind, tolerant, patient, and compassionate to have these

---

[20] Dr. Ernest Holmes, Religious Science, The Science of Mind textbook 1938

kinds of experiences. In other words, if you embrace these loving ideas about yourself and your world, your health will be restored to you.

You need to love yourself and **act as if** you are **Worthy and Deserving** of the very best of everything that life has to offer. Get off your back! Stop analyzing and judging yourself for everything that is wrong in your life.

Start focusing on what is **right in your life**. Start focusing on what you have to be **thankful for**. Be thankful and **grateful** for all your **blessings**, and make room for more of them. Whatever you believe about yourself will manifest in your life. So we need to **BE conscious** of our thoughts. We need to **BE conscious** of the Words that come out of our mouth.

We need to **Love** ourselves unconditionally and

without judgment. I can't say this enough. If you

can embrace this you will **Love** yourself into health,

into wealth, into loving relationships and into the

most fantastic creative expression.

I do believe there is a **Power for Good** in the

Universe. I call this **Power God**. And I recognize

that **I Am** the **Beloved. I Am created** in the

image and likeness of **God** and so are **You!**

With this recognition of **Who** you truly are,

a **Spiritual Being**, you become Empowered to the

knowing that you can live your life as you choose.

Affirmations for your Life Areas

These affirmations will be most effective if you get
yourself in a relaxed state. Focus on your breathing
and think about your **Higher Power** within. Then say
the Affirmation out loud for the **Life Area** that you need for
the day.

The following four Spiritual affirmations are from
Creative Thought magazine, a publication
of Religious Science International, September 2004
and February 2005 editions.

Health

"I Embody a Healing Consciousness

There is One Love, One Law, and One Healing

Power- the One God. It is All Good, and I am an

effect of this First Cause, the Absolute Spirit of the

Universe. I know my body is an effect, and with

delight and wonder, I ponder this thought. As an

effect of First Cause, it is only possible that I am

perfect, for only good and perfect creations come

from this Oneness.

As I celebrate this day, I celebrate my body as the

wondrous vehicle with which I am flowing through

life. I embrace abundant good as I realize the depth

of my health. I breathe in deeply and recognize my

perfection. Any thought of disease has departed as I

take in this magnificence of me, the absolute divine being I

am.

I am grateful for my perfectly whole and healthy body. I am grateful for my life. I release my word to Divine Consciousness, to the Oneness that made me, for it is already done. And so it is".

(Gail Ingwall, R.Sc.P. Toronto, ON)

Wealth or Abundance

"I Partake of Infinite Supply

There is One Divine Power, One Infinite Energy,

One Creator called God. It is the Source, supply, and

Substance of my life. I realize I am one with this

Divine presence, and I awaken to the realization that

I am powerful and divine, unlimited and creative.

With this Truth in mind, I tap into the abundance of

the Universe. As I release my full potential, good

flows into my life effortlessly. This is the beginning of

a new way of living, and I delight in its beauty. My

heart is open, and I grasp the opportunities that

come my way. In my financial affairs, I receive the

flow of money from many sources, expected and

unexpected, and I am thankful.

Grateful for wealth, love, joy, and peace of mind, I

am free. I release my work to the Law of Mind, and it

returns to me as greater and greater abundance. I

let go and let God. And so it is".

(Rev. Barbara Schreiner-Trudel, Toronto, ON)

Love

"I Experience Love Always

God's Love, within me, is me. I am eternally in the
Presence of Spirit, and Spirit uses me as a channel of
Its Love. I do not have to earn God's Love; It simply
is. As I turn my awareness to the Presence, I make a
new choice to allow myself to perceive and
experience Divine Love within and through me in all ways.

Knowing I am one with Spirit, I now attract the
experience of love. God's Love filters into all my
relationships and activities. Acknowledging the
Divine Love within, I love myself. Creating an aura of
love, I attract loving people in my life. I share this
good with others, and they respond from the eternal
well of God's Love within them.

I am open and receptive to new and creative ways to express my love, and my world expands without limit. I relax in the warmth and radiance of Spirit with gratitude for Its eternal Presence. I know this is the Truth for me now".

(Alice Gravelle Kann, R.Sc.P. Montvale, NJ)

Creative Expression

"Perfect Fulfillment Is Mine

There is One Divine Creative Action and Activity in the Universe. It is God's Activity, and it is truly wonderful. Because I am a unique and perfect individualization of God, I now manifest this creativity in my life.

I am always in the place I love to be, doing that which I love in an atmosphere of joy. New, creative ideas are always coming to me to be expressed and circulated in my world, with ease, for the good and delight of all people. I accept these ideas with gratitude and empower them with my consciousness of love. New, greater, and more glorious expressions of Sprit are appearing in my world, and the glory of God shines through my success.

In complete ease, I accept abundant compensation and recognition for that which I do, and I am totally fulfilled. Any patterns of worry, frustration, or fear are dissolved from my consciousness in peace as I now manifest greatness. I rejoice that this is the truth of my being. And so it is".

(Rev. C.C. Banks, White Plains, NY)

The Word

"The Word is the concept, Idea, Image, or Thought of God. It is the Self-Knowing Mind, speaking itself into manifestation".[21]

The Word is the mold that decides what form the thought to take. It is very important that we become aware of how **Powerful** our **Word** is. Always remember, that, "**what ever you put out comes back**". So pay careful attention to the Words you speak, to yourselves, and everyone else.

Understand that life is your mirror. And if you are angry, or hostile or abusive to someone, it is really you that you are attacking.

The more completely we believe in the **Power** of our **spoken Words**, the more **Power** our Words will

---

[21] Dr. Ernest Holmes, Religious Science, The Science of Mind textbook 1938

---

have. The greater the **consciousness**, the more **Power** our Words will have.

When we speak our Words with **Power**, it activates the **Spiritual Scientific Healing Formula** in the subconscious side of our life. This results in conditions or effects that manifest in our life. This is an example of **Cause and Effect**.

We want to make sure the conditions or effects that show up are truly what we want. So we have to **speak** our **Words** with **Life Affirming ideas**.

The Power of Intention

Your **desire** is what sets the **Power of Intention** into motion. **Attitude** goes along with the Power of Intention. When you realize **Who** you are, and you become **Empowered** through your thoughts, feelings, and emotions, to consciously make choices, then you develop an attitude about yourself and life.

You recognize that there is a **Power** for **Good, God,** and you set your Power of Intention for what you want to co-create and express.

I came across a great article about the Power of Intention by, Joel Garfinkle, Dream Job Coaching
"Every action starts with an idea followed by the intention to take action upon that idea. Edison may very well have first considered the idea of a steady light source because reading by oil lamp was difficult

and unsatisfactory. And, if he intended to create a new light source, he may have surmised it would also be great if the light was available at the flick of a switch. The leap between idea and intention does not guarantee instant success. It took Edison several thousand tries before he successfully came up with the electric light. But success came only after he made the conscious decision to achieve/create something. The power of intention will help lead you to success.

You are a powerful, magnificent, wonderful and passionate being. This is your true essence. Yet, most of us see ourselves as less. Why do we spend our days focusing on what we can't do, who we can't be, the challenges we won't overcome and the dreams we won't achieve? The answer lies in our intentions. Because of its great ability to accomplish amazing results, intention and action must be directed toward results to maximize your results.

This is called the power of intention.

When I started my business, Dream Job Coaching, I felt powerful and powerless. The feelings of power occurred when I gained more clarity of my vision for my company, enjoyed the rewards of great friendships, attracted new clients from my target market, collaborated with other creative and bright coaches and organized my office space to be more efficient. I felt on top of the world. I was able to expand my dreams for the future. My power of intention was focused on this manifestation.

After this great beginning, my power of intention became redirected because of my frustration at the lack of freedom I was feeling. As my dream business took off, I had less time to devote to planning new programs and ancillary materials for my business. Once I became focused on the negative feelings, time constraints decreased my freedom. I started paying attention to the negative voices inside me, "I can't do it. I'm not worthy of attracting all these gifts and I don't have the power to innovate." These voices of doubt and fear overcame the great burst of energy that I felt in the previous weeks and my productivity plummeted.

The difference between one week's doubt and another week's successes is where I focused my power of intention. I took my attention off my doubts and placed it on how to grow and improve my business. I generated power by taking constructive action steps. In short, I redirected my power of intention. Now, after this tough period of feeling powerful and then powerless, I believe in myself again, my dreams, and my ability to create and manifest all that I am in the world.

Changing the direction of your power of intention can change your feelings and your results. You might have the habit of allowing yourself to get caught up in negative feelings. Usually when this happens, your energy is diverted to those negative feelings and away from taking constructive steps, especially the

challenging, scary ones, to attain your goals. A coach, friend or any understanding individual can offer you the support to get through the self-doubts and assist you in redirecting your power of intention toward achieving your goals.

Putting the power of intention to work means being focused on what is best for you and having a clear idea of how you're going to achieve it. Then, once you have an objective and a strategy, take action! Action is the only way to move your desired result from being out there to reality. As one of my clients said about the power of intention, "when one focuses on achieving a particular result, and acknowledges a process leading to an objective, one fuels the process and things get done very quickly."

Keep taking risks and moving the comfort zone beyond where you are comfortable. Notice the gifts that come your way. One day, you'll have accomplished your dreams and realized it was the power of intention that moved you there. Henry Miller said, "The moment one gives close attention to anything, even a blade a grass, it becomes a mysterious, awesome, indescribably magnificent world unto itself."[22]

---

[22] Joel Garfinkle - http://www.dreamjobcoaching.com/resources/articles/the-power-of-intention/

Parents

Parents, when dealing with your children, **Love them Unconditionally, without Judgment**. Let them know that you honor their journey.

Teach them that they create their own reality by the choices that they make. Teach them the **Principles of "cause and effect"**, and "**It is done unto you as you believe"**. Help them to understand that they are accountable for their actions, just as you are. Do what you can to help them. If they are being destructive, **Love** them unconditionally. Give them a **Spiritual Scientific Healing prayer** for **Divine Right Action**.

Hold up a mirror for them so that they see who they are destroying. And most importantly, set a good example for them to learn from.

If they see that their parents are not loving and are being destructive, they will learn the wrong messages. Respect their beingness, their identity.

Treat them as adults with your communications. This means to communicate from Adult to Adult as opposed to Adult to Child. Encourage them to express their feelings and take ownership for those feelings.

Encourage them to communicate. If not to you, then to a neutral third party. Respect their right to live their life as they choose.

I heard Dr. Wayne Dyer tell a story of how an indigenous tribe treats its members that become unruly and destructive to one another.

All the tribe members get to express themselves to the unruly one. But not in the manner that we Westerners do.

Rather, they all have their turn telling the unruly one how important and **Loved** he is and what he means to them individually and collectively to the tribe.

This can go on for days, depending on the size of the tribe. It is non-stop until everyone has their turn. I believe the children are included.

When it is all done, then there is a celebration to invite the unruly one back into the tribe as a loving member.

WOW! - Can you imagine if we tried this with our children? This is an example of unconditional love at its highest form, without judgment. We need to open our minds to new ideas and ways of communicating with our children. Treat them as we would like to be treated if the situation was reversed.

As Little Children interpreted (Matt. 18:3)

"We must become as little children. How we long for a
return of that simple trust in life which children have; in their
minds there are no doubts-they have not yet been told that
they are sinners, destitute of divine guidance and spiritual life.
The life of the child is lived in natural goodness. God is natural
goodness.

The prison walls of false experience soon build themselves
into barriers, shutting out the light, and the child grows into a
man, often losing his sense of that inner Guide, leading his
footsteps aright".

"We must return the way we came. As little children,

who know that life is good and to be trusted, we are

to approach our problems as though they were not.

Approaching them in this manner, they will vanish".

"Let not the materialists deny us this right, nor the

unbelieving cast any reflection of his blindness before our

eyes. There is a wisdom and power not of the flesh, which

rings perennially from the innerlife-all powerful and all-

wise". [23]

---

[23] Dr. Ernest Holmes, Religious Science, The Science of Mind textbook 1938

I love the above! It is this **"innocence"** that I seek.
The wonderful, carefree time, before we had judgments about ourselves and other people.

My **natural child** is the lead character for me. I **Love** being in touch with it. The natural child to me represents the time when the "armor of the warrior" is removed and you can let your self "just be" **Who** you are. It is a time when you are **one with life** and **everything flows**. I guess it might be analogous to the athlete or artist "being in the zone".
It is the time when we can just let our defenses down and be totally vulnerable to life.

"We do not stop playing because we grow old;
we grow old because we stop playing".[24]

"Don't let an old person grow in your body".

---

[24] http://www.naturalchild.org/

Spiritual Scientific Healing Formula

Every day I do my **Spiritual Scientific Healing**

work to recognize Myself. This is a form of Prayer.

It is not beseeching any Power outside me.

This form of positive prayer follows these **five steps**:

1. **Recognizing** who **I AM**. **I AM** the **Beloved**.

2. **Unify** with this Power that runs the Universe and my Life.

3. I **Declare** what I want, and Act As If my desire is already accomplished.

4. I **Give Thanks** for it already being done.

5. **Release** my **Spiritual Scientific Healing** Prayer

to Universal Mind for the Spiritual Law to take place.

This Releasing also goes by the name of Letting

Go or Surrendering to the Power within you.

You too can do this!

Spiritual Scientific Healing for a Loved One

I now declare that my son, ___ (fill in the appropriate name), is **Perfect, Whole** and **Complete** in everyway.

The same healing and loving energy that I feel right this moment is the same healing and loving energy that run's through ____. I declare that **Divine Right Action** is now guiding ____ to make the right decisions that Now bring him **Peace, Love, Joy** and wonderful **vibrant health, great prosperity, creative self-expression** and great **Love.**

And now release this into the Universe by saying,

With great **Thanksgiving** and acceptance as already done,

So It Is.

Make time for You

It is very important that you make time for yourself everyday to "get quiet" and centered.

Free yourself from all your external distractions. If you can create a little space that is just your space, all the better.

The purpose of this is to get quiet so you can hear yourself think. See what is on your mind. See what you are in touch with. What are you feeling?

Focus on your breath. Do some deep breathing to get yourself quiet.

When you are quiet, think about **Who** you are and your **Spiritual connection** to life.

It would help if you could make the time in the morning shortly after awakening to do some **Spiritual** reading. It does not matter how much time, but just develop the habit. At night time, after you get into your bed and before you fall asleep, give **thanks for the day's blessings**.

Rebuild your Self-Esteem, Image and Worth

I know we talked about this earlier, but it is so important that it needs additional words.

Low Self Esteem creates a poor self image, so our outlook on life is not joyful.
We have to be conscious of the self-sabotage type of thoughts that we have. This is where we think we want something and our feelings and emotions contradict it.

I am discovering that the words that come out of my mouth are not necessarily what I believe.

Get quiet with yourself and connect to **Spirit**. With your **Power of Intention**, your **desire, declare** to yourself that **what you want is already done**. And then Image it; feel what it would feel like to experience what you want.

Really embellish upon all the feelings.

Paint a grand picture in your mind's eye.

What does this have to with your self image?

Everything, If you don't feel **worthy** or **deserving**

of what you want, you won't get it.

Affirmations are great. Make up your own,

and **Act As If.**

For example:

I AM worthy and **deserving** of the very best of

everything that life has to offer. **I AM** the **rich child**

of a **loving God** and **I claim my good.**

Tools - Micro Cassette Recorder

Buy yourself a little micro cassette recorder with tapes. When you are through with your quiet time and you are centered spiritually, make a personal recording for yourself. There is nothing more powerful than for you to hear your own voice telling you how wonderful you are.

Make a recording for yourself, which you can use when you get into bed. Put it on right as you are starting to fall asleep. Make a recording that tells you **Who** you are, what kind of human being you are. For example:

Mary, You are the Beloved. You are **created** in the **image** and **likeness** of **God**. You are a **Spiritual Being** that has been given the **Power of Choice.** Mary, you are a wonderful, loving human being. You are loving wife, a loving Mother, a great friend, etc. fill it in, keep going.

When you are done with this part, then pick something from one of your **Life Areas** that you want to change. In another words, **what is your greatest desire?**

For example, I want to creatively express myself as an artist. So on your recording, say something like: "Mary, through the Power of your choice, You claim that your artistic endeavor, (say it specifically), is now giving expression through you. You are an artist, doing _____, and loving it. Your creative expression feels so good. You are expressing yourself beyond your wildest dreams".

Embellish about how it feels. Feel satisfied, fulfilled and happy. See yourself making lots of money at it. **Act As If** it is already done.

The **Mind** only knows the moment and the subconscious doesn't know the difference between what is real and what is imaginary.

Give great **Thanks**, for this already being done and now **release** it to the **Law of Mind**. And to conclude and accept, you say, "And So It is!".

Do this every night and see how things start to change for you. Remember "**it is done unto you as you believe**". So you have to believe that is working for you.

Meditation

"describes a state of concentrated attention on some object of thought or awareness. It usually involves turning the attention inward to the mind itself. Meditation is often recognized as a component of Eastern religions, where it has been practiced for over 5,000 years. It has also become mainstream in Western culture. It encompasses any of a wide variety of spiritual practices which emphasize mental activity or quiescence. Meditation can be used for personal development, or to focus the mind on God (or an aspect of God).

Meditation is usually defined as one of the following:

A state of relaxed concentration on the reality of the present moment.

A state that is experienced when the mind dissolves and is free of all thoughts.

Concentration in which the attention has been liberated from restlessness and is focused on God.

A mental "opening up" to the divine, invoking the guidance of a higher power".[25]

---

[25] 25 http://en.wikipedia.org/wiki/Meditation The Free Encyclopedia

Free Healing Meditation

"Find a comfortable space, either sit or lie in a

relaxed position. As you become settled, begin to

focus on your breath. Inhale, then exhale at a

comfortable pace – an even breath.

Close your eyes.

Continue your rhythmic breathing. If you become

distracted refocus on your breath.

As you sink into comfort and relaxation, see yourself

basking in a waterfall of sunlight and crystal clear water.

As the sun and water cascade over your body you

absorb the healing oxygen carried within your blood

vessels though your whole system.

The oxygen heals and releases the holding

contraction of each muscle. Each muscle becomes

taffy… soft and pliable.

All tension gives way to relaxation. The cascade of sunshine

reminds you of the source of all energy.

Your whole being sings with release and renewal as

the source refuels and fortifies your body and spirit.

In healing all is possible. As you heal your spirit and body your gifts to the universe emerge.

Your loving compassion explodes for sharing with your fellow travelers. As you heal yourself you heal all who cross your path. Your connection to others heals as you move to your new level of evolution.

You are the incarnation of universal healing. It begins with you.

The healing vision of cascading sunshine and water is yours whenever you want it to be. Come back to this space whenever you want to, know that this space is always available even for a moment. Be aware once again of your breath. Inhale... exhale as your re-enter the space around you. Open your eyes and carry your renewed energy to all with whom you come in contact".[26]

LifeWorks

LifeWorks are what most people call coincidence or luck. I choose to think of it as **Synchronicities**. There are different definitions for Synchronicities.

http://en.wikipedia.org/wiki/Synchronicity

My definition is that when you are in alignment with your higher self, the Universe mirrors back to you what you need, and provides for you without any sense of struggle. I guess you could say that these are the everyday Miracles.

You know, the way that Life is supposed to work.

Ralph Waldo Emerson said,

"Let us take our bloated nothingness out of the path of the divine circuits."

Below are a couple of my **LifeWorks**. Feel free to email me yours, so we can share with others.

At the annual RSI Asilomar conference, I wanted to

buy a book from a recent seminar that I attended. I waited too long to go to the bookstore. When I had seen the author on the pathway I told her I was going to the bookstore to buy her book and asked her if she would like to autograph it. She replied she was sorry but the books were all sold out and she proceeded to tell me what bookstores I could go to. That same day on the steps on the administration building, I was talking with Rev. Joyce Franz who told me she had just bought the book that I wanted and that she didn't know why she bought it. She asked if I would like to have it.

This is a **LifeWorks**- when you need something, and let it be known, the Universe finds a way to give it to you.

I had some computer books that I no longer needed. I went to my office and got a box for them. I had planned to take them to a special rehab center that my wife and I donate to. I came home, brought the box upstairs, put the books in and got ready to to put them in my car. My wife told me that our

spiritual center is having a used book sale and would

like to have the books. That night we dropped them off.

Do you see what is happening here?

A few months ago Bette Midler was coming to town

and I really wanted to see her perform. There are

very few entertainers I am interested in seeing and

she is one of them. When I found out she was

coming to town, it was after the fact. It appeared

that the shows were sold out. The next day a friend

of mine told me Bette was adding one more show

because she had sold out so quickly. I immediately

called, waited a long time on the phone to get a

ticket agent, and then began getting the details. The

agent said there were few tickets left and oh boy I

got two. The only catch was due to a lack of time I

would have to pick up the tickets the night of the

show and that meant long lines, I was turned off big

time and canceled. Remember the Universe provides for us, so even though I was disappointed, I let go of this idea.

Now it is a few months later and guess where I am going next week. You guessed it, Bette Midler decided to come back to town and I got great seats, hand delivered.

At work, I was asked to find out about the Siemens companies in my territory. I knew I had done this before and did not learn anything that would be of help. Then a few days had passed and my wife and I went out to lunch together. Lo and behold, the woman at the next table was talking loud and telling her friend that she worked at one of the Siemens locations and provided me with enough information to know something was going on that I did not know about.

Now it is your turn- send me your **LifeWorks**. These **LifeWork** situations happen everyday and in everyone's life. These are the **everyday Miracles** we miss until we become conscious of them.

Suggested Readings

http://raymondcharlesbarker.wwwhubs.com/

http://emilecoue.wwwhubs.com/

http://emmetfox.wwwhubs.com/

http://napoleonhill.wwwhubs.com/

http://ernestholmes.wwwhubs.com/

http://josephmurphy.wwwhubs.com/

http://normanvincentpeale.wwwhubs.com/

http://catherineponder.wwwhubs.com/

http://cornerstone.wwwhubs.com/pos.html

(Brian Tracy)

http://thomastroward.wwwhubs.com/

http://phineasquimby.wwwhubs.com/

http://shaktigawain.wwwhubs.com/

http://louisehay.wwwhubs.com/

http://deepakchopra.wwwhubs.com/

http://stuartgrayson.wwwhubs.com/

http://garyzukav.wwwhubs.com/

http://waynedyer.wwwhubs.com/

http://edwenegaines.wwwhubs.com/

http://en.wikipedia.org/wiki/Michael_Talbot (Holographic Universe)

http://www.dosseydossey.com/larry/book.html

http://www.mindperk.com/Maltz.htm (Maxwell Maltz-Psycho-Cybernetics)

http://www.berniesiegelmd.com/

http://www.brianweiss.com/index.htm

http://www.dalailama.com/

http://borysenko.powersource3.com/tapebook/index.cfm#Anchor-BOOKS-49575

http://www.ananda.org/ananda/yogananda.html

Summary

People all over the Globe are starting to awaken and realize there must be something better than the state that we are in, mentally spiritually, emotionally and physically. We are starting to have a shift in consciousness from Competition, to **Compassion and Service**. We have to understand the **Spiritual Scientific Healing Principles** that govern the Universe and align ourselves with them. And we have to believe them. **"It is done unto you as you believe"**

Do you believe this?

Or do you just think that things happen to you randomly or by coincidence or by accident? Or by Luck- **(logical use of conscious knowledge)**

The Master teacher said,

"**to Love God with all your Heart, Soul and Mind and Love your neighbor as yourself**". [27]

So we have **Love and Law**. The application of the

Spiritual Scientific Healing Principles are the

Law. This book is for your journey and to

the understanding that life is a Mirror.

It Mirrors back to you who you are. Everything in

your life that you perceive with your senses are all

effects. These effects are your Mirror to see what

you believe about yourself.

Remember that what you think and what you believe

will not necessarily be the same thing.

Look at what is in your **Life Areas** to determine

what you believe.

---

[27] King James Bible (Matt. 22: 37-40

If you are interested in working with me, one on one, I will write a specific **Spiritual Scientific Healing Prayer** for **You**. It is based on the **Spiritual Scientific Healing Formula** discussed earlier in this book. It will help you eliminate and replace a condition or effect in your life that you would like to change. This will take place after our initial **FREE** consultation. During our consultation, I get to learn **Who** you are, and we will share ideas that will foster your growth.

Please visit my website first, it is www.mindmattersinc.biz and then email me at jedzim@mindmattersinc.biz

Epilogue

Our whole way of life is in dis-repair.

Our economic system is broken.

Our education system is broken.

Our medical system is broken.

Our family life system is broken.

Our Government is broken.

Mother Earth is on the mend. When we see what she is doing, we call them **Acts of God**. I believe that to be true. I believe an awakening is underway. But we need the critical mass to be a part of this awakening.

Mankind, (including Womankind) need to accept ownership and responsibility for their actions.

We were given **Free Will** - the **Power of Choice**.

Until Man **feels** the results of his actions, and makes the **connection**, that what he puts out has to come back, (**Cause and Effect**), life will not change for the better.

Because of the **illusion of time**, Man does not make the connection of what his actions produce. Some men lie, cheat, steal, rape and kill. They are motivated by their greed and conflict of interest.

They think because they don't get caught, they can get away with these actions. The **Universe is never debtor**. The **Spiritual Scientific Healing Principles** are **absolute**. They always work.
We can never, never get away with anything that harms another human being.

Nothing in the Universe happens by **accident** or coincidence. We just don't understand.

We are all **Connected**! We are all in the University of Life together. We need to change our ways.

It is our **Divine Birthright**, to be **Healthy**, to be **Wealthy**, to be **Loving** and to be **Creative**.
If we align ourselves with the **Spiritual Scientific Healing Principles** that govern the Universe, we will be it all and have it all.

God bless us all!

www.ingramcontent.com/pod-product-compliance
Lightning Source LLC
Chambersburg PA
CBHW021342090426
42742CB00008B/699